100 Ways to Change the World,
One Good Deed at a Time!

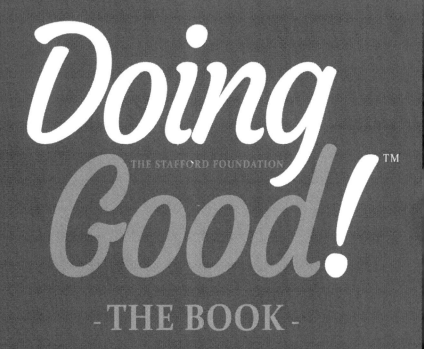

THE STAFFORD FOUNDATION

Doing
Good!
-THE BOOK-

™

THE STAFFORD FOUNDATION

Thank you for picking up a copy of The Doing Good book. We want to hear from you!

Please send your questions or comments about this book to us at
info@TheStaffordFoundation.org

Contributing Authors: (in alphabetical order)
Robin Forrest, Rania Nazhat, Joe Paul, Earl W. Stafford, Mark Stafford, Brooke Watson

Cover and interior design:
Joe Paul

The Doing Good Book

ISBN: 978-0-578-58420-1

This book is dedicated to everyone who has ever done something for someone else and expected nothing in return. The world needs more angels like you.

This book is also dedicated to the countless volunteers who offer their time, treasure, talent or a combination of the three to giving back to individuals and families in need.

For more information on how to get involved and ways you can give back to The Stafford Foundation, please visit www.DoingGood.com

Visit The Doing Good online store to show your support in style! 100% of the proceeds support our programs and initiatives.

Shop The Doing Good Store

https://doing-good-store.myshopify.com/

Our Mission

The Stafford Foundation is a charitable organization based on the principles of Jesus Christ with a glocal mission of helping others to help themselves.

Our Vision

We envision a world in which all people will have the opportunity to become self-reliant and live in dignity.

A history of The Stafford Foundation doing good for others

The Stafford Foundation believes in doing good for others. For more than a decade, the foundation's gifts and programs have impacted more than a quarter of a million lives from across the world. We've empowered the homeless to help themselves and designed robust programs to assist women and children in need. Join us in changing the world, one good deed at a time.

www.TheStaffordFoundation.org

What does it mean to do good?

Doing Good is treating others in need the way you would want to be treated.

Why is Doing Good important?

Doing good and helping others can make an enormous impact on their sense of self-esteem and self-worth.

How does Doing Good change lives and communities?

Doing good involves paying it forward and giving without the expectation of getting anything in return.

The Doing Good Book

100 Ways to Change the World, One Good Deed at a Time!

The Stafford Foundation

Doing Good Deed #1:

Volunteer one hour of your time at a local homeless shelter.

My Doing Good Journal
Doing Good Deed #1

Date Completed: _____

What did you learn from this experience?

_____

_____

_____

_____

_____

_____

_____

_____

Doing Good Deed #2:

Invite an elderly neighbor to lunch or offer to bring them a warm meal.

My Doing Good Journal
Doing Good Deed #2

Date Completed: _____

What did you learn from this experience?

_____

_____

_____

_____

_____

_____

_____

_____

Doing Good Deed #3:

Donate gently used clothing to your local shelter or Salvation Army.

My Doing Good Journal
Doing Good Deed #3

Date Completed: _____

What did you learn from this experience?

_____

_____

_____

_____

_____

_____

_____

_____

Doing Good Deed #4:

Create a canned food drive amongst friends and donate it to your local food bank.

My Doing Good Journal
Doing Good Deed #4

Date Completed: _____

What did you learn from this experience?

_____

_____

_____

_____

_____

_____

_____

_____

Doing Good Deed #5:

Purchase groceries for the person ahead of you in line.

My Doing Good Journal
Doing Good Deed #5

Date Completed: _____

What did you learn from this experience?

_____

_____

_____

_____

_____

_____

_____

_____

Doing Good Deed #6:

Purchase school supplies for a child in need.

My Doing Good Journal
Doing Good Deed #6

Date Completed: _____

What did you learn from this experience?

_____

_____

_____

_____

_____

_____

_____

_____

Doing Good Deed #7:

Offer to wash an elderly or disabled neighbor's car.

My Doing Good Journal
Doing Good Deed #7

Date Completed: _____

What did you learn from this experience?

_____

_____

_____

_____

_____

_____

_____

_____

Doing Good Deed #8:

Volunteer at a local soup kitchen.

My Doing Good Journal
Doing Good Deed #8

Date Completed: _____

What did you learn from this experience?

_____

_____

_____

_____

_____

_____

_____

_____

Doing Good Deed #9:

Donate pet food and supplies to an animal shelter.

My Doing Good Journal
Doing Good Deed #9

Date Completed: _____

What did you learn from this experience?

_____

_____

_____

_____

_____

_____

_____

_____

Doing Good Deed #10:

Offer to walk your elderly or disabled neighbors' pet.

My Doing Good Journal
Doing Good Deed #10

Date Completed: _____

What did you learn from this experience?

_____

_____

_____

_____

_____

_____

_____

_____

Doing Good Deed #11:

Share the principles of Jesus Christ with someone.

My Doing Good Journal
Doing Good Deed #11

Date Completed: _____

What did you learn from this experience?

_____

_____

_____

_____

_____

_____

_____

_____

Doing Good Deed #12:

Purchase a gift card for a complete stranger.

My Doing Good Journal
Doing Good Deed #12

Date Completed: _____

What did you learn from this experience?

_____

_____

_____

_____

_____

_____

_____

Doing Good Deed #13:

Volunteer your time at a public school.

My Doing Good Journal
Doing Good Deed #13

Date Completed: _____

What did you learn from this experience?

_____

_____

_____

_____

_____

_____

_____

_____

Doing Good Deed #14:

Read to children at your local library.

My Doing Good Journal
Doing Good Deed #14

Date Completed: _____

What did you learn from this experience?

_____

_____

_____

_____

_____

_____

_____

_____

Doing Good Deed #15:

Volunteer to help clean the house of an elderly or disabled person.

My Doing Good Journal
Doing Good Deed #15

Date Completed: _____

What did you learn from this experience?

_____

_____

_____

_____

_____

_____

_____

_____

Doing Good Deed #16:

Take baked goods or healthy snacks to a local fire station.

My Doing Good Journal
Doing Good Deed #16

Date Completed: _____

What did you learn from this experience?

_____

_____

_____

_____

_____

_____

_____

Doing Good Deed #17:

Volunteer your time at a Special Olympics event.

My Doing Good Journal
Doing Good Deed #17

Date Completed: _____

What did you learn from this experience?

_____

_____

_____

_____

_____

_____

_____

_____

Doing Good Deed #18:

Participate in a walk or race to raise awareness for a cause.

My Doing Good Journal
Doing Good Deed #18

Date Completed: _____

What did you learn from this experience?

_____

_____

_____

_____

_____

_____

_____

_____

Doing Good Deed #19:

Have a yard sale and donate the proceeds to a good cause or charity.

My Doing Good Journal
Doing Good Deed #19

Date Completed: _____

What did you learn from this experience?

_____

_____

_____

_____

_____

_____

_____

_____

Doing Good Deed #20:

Volunteer your time at a nursing home and make a new friend.

My Doing Good Journal
Doing Good Deed #20

Date Completed: _____

What did you learn from this experience?

_____

_____

_____

_____

_____

_____

_____

_____

Doing Good Deed #21:

Send holiday or thank you cards to military personnel serving overseas.

My Doing Good Journal
Doing Good Deed #21

Date Completed: _____

What did you learn from this experience?

_____

_____

_____

_____

_____

_____

_____

_____

Doing Good Deed #22:

Start a blanket drive for the homeless and donate them to a local shelter.

My Doing Good Journal
Doing Good Deed #22

Date Completed: _____

What did you learn from this experience?

_____

_____

_____

_____

_____

_____

_____

_____

Doing Good Deed #23:

Anonymously pay for a stranger's meal at a restaurant.

My Doing Good Journal
Doing Good Deed #23

Date Completed: _____

What did you learn from this experience?

_____

_____

_____

_____

_____

_____

_____

_____

Doing Good Deed #24:

Leave a bonus tip for good service.

My Doing Good Journal
Doing Good Deed #24

Date Completed: _____

What did you learn from this experience?

_____

_____

_____

_____

_____

_____

_____

_____

Doing Good Deed #25:

Volunteer your time at a Veterans Administration hospital.

My Doing Good Journal
Doing Good Deed #25

Date Completed: _____

What did you learn from this experience?

_____

_____

_____

_____

_____

_____

_____

_____

Doing Good Deed #26:

Work with a school to sponsor a pizza party for a class recognized for community service.

My Doing Good Journal
Doing Good Deed #26

Date Completed: _____

What did you learn from this experience?

_____

_____

_____

_____

_____

_____

_____

_____

Doing Good Deed #27:

Give a gift card to the next cashier you meet.

My Doing Good Journal
Doing Good Deed #27

Date Completed: _____

What did you learn from this experience?

_____

_____

_____

_____

_____

_____

_____

_____

Doing Good Deed #28:

Donate shoes and
sneakers to an
international charity
like Soles4Souls.org

My Doing Good Journal
Doing Good Deed #28

Date Completed: _____

What did you learn from this experience?

_____

_____

_____

_____

_____

_____

_____

_____

Doing Good Deed #29:

Participate in a community enhancement project.

My Doing Good Journal
Doing Good Deed #29

Date Completed: _____

What did you learn from this experience?

_____

_____

_____

_____

_____

_____

_____

_____

Doing Good Deed #30:

Donate funds to a veteran's program or the Wounded Warriors Project®.

My Doing Good Journal
Doing Good Deed #30

Date Completed: _____

What did you learn from this experience?

_____

_____

_____

_____

_____

_____

_____

_____

Doing Good Deed #31:

Purchase a case of water online for a church or charitable organization in Flint, Michigan.

My Doing Good Journal
Doing Good Deed #31

Date Completed: _____

What did you learn from this experience?

_____

_____

_____

_____

_____

_____

_____

_____

Doing Good Deed #32:

Send a care package to our men and women serving overseas.

(www.uso.org)

My Doing Good Journal
Doing Good Deed #32

Date Completed: _____

What did you learn from this experience?

_____

_____

_____

_____

_____

_____

_____

_____

Doing Good Deed #33:

Pay for an expired parking meter.

My Doing Good Journal
Doing Good Deed #33

Date Completed: _____

What did you learn from this experience?

_____

_____

_____

_____

_____

_____

_____

Doing Good Deed #34:

Offer to pay for a load of laundry for a stranger at a laundromat.

My Doing Good Journal
Doing Good Deed #34

Date Completed: _____

What did you learn from this experience?

_____

_____

_____

_____

_____

_____

_____

Doing Good Deed #35:

Donate books to your local library.

My Doing Good Journal
Doing Good Deed #35

Date Completed: _____

What did you learn from this experience?

_____

_____

_____

_____

_____

_____

_____

_____

Doing Good Deed #36:

Invite someone to attend a local church with you.

My Doing Good Journal
Doing Good Deed #36

Date Completed: _____

What did you learn from this experience?

_____

_____

_____

_____

_____

_____

_____

_____

Doing Good Deed #37:

Buy a gift for a single mother - just because.

My Doing Good Journal
Doing Good Deed #37

Date Completed: _____

What did you learn from this experience?

_____

_____

_____

_____

_____

_____

_____

_____

Doing Good Deed #38:

Teach an elderly person how to use the internet, social media and write emails.

My Doing Good Journal
Doing Good Deed #38

Date Completed: _____

What did you learn from this experience?

_____

_____

_____

_____

_____

_____

_____

Doing Good Deed #39:

Collect stuffed animals and donate them to an organization that assists children.

My Doing Good Journal
Doing Good Deed #39

Date Completed: _____

What did you learn from this experience?

_____

_____

_____

_____

_____

_____

_____

_____

Doing Good Deed #40:

Participate in an Adopt-A-Block or community clean-up project.

My Doing Good Journal
Doing Good Deed #40

Date Completed: _____

What did you learn from this experience?

_____

_____

_____

_____

_____

_____

_____

_____

Doing Good Deed #41:

Offer to read to residents in a nursing home or rehabilitation center.

My Doing Good Journal
Doing Good Deed #41

Date Completed: _____

What did you learn from this experience?

_____

_____

_____

_____

_____

_____

_____

_____

Doing Good Deed #42:

Take part in a literacy program for children to enhance their reading skills.

My Doing Good Journal
Doing Good Deed #42

Date Completed: _____

What did you learn from this experience?

_____

_____

_____

_____

_____

_____

_____

_____

Doing Good Deed #43:

Collect duffle bags and suitcases and donate them to a foster care program.

My Doing Good Journal
Doing Good Deed #43

Date Completed: _____

What did you learn from this experience?

_____

_____

_____

_____

_____

_____

_____

_____

Doing Good Deed #44:

Take food or dessert to welcome a new neighbor.

My Doing Good Journal
Doing Good Deed #44

Date Completed: _____

What did you learn from this experience?

_____

_____

_____

_____

_____

_____

_____

_____

Doing Good Deed #45:

Treat an underprivileged family to dinner or an entertainment event.

My Doing Good Journal
Doing Good Deed #45

Date Completed: _____

What did you learn from this experience?

_____

_____

_____

_____

_____

_____

_____

_____

Doing Good Deed #46:

Collect small soaps and toiletries and donate them to a battered women's shelter.

My Doing Good Journal
Doing Good Deed #46

Date Completed: _____

What did you learn from this experience?

_____

_____

_____

_____

_____

_____

_____

_____

Doing Good Deed #47:

Next time you're out buying food, purchase an extra item and give it to a homeless person.

My Doing Good Journal
Doing Good Deed #47

Date Completed: _____

What did you learn from this experience?

_____

_____

_____

_____

_____

_____

_____

_____

Doing Good Deed #48:

Volunteer to help start a community garden and donate the harvest to a food bank.

My Doing Good Journal
Doing Good Deed #48

Date Completed: _____

What did you learn from this experience?

_____

_____

_____

_____

_____

_____

_____

_____

Doing Good Deed #49:

Bring a meal to someone who is at home recovering from surgery or an illness.

My Doing Good Journal
Doing Good Deed #49

Date Completed: _____

What did you learn from this experience?

_____

_____

_____

_____

_____

_____

_____

_____

Doing Good Deed #50:

Donate blood or volunteer your time to the American Red Cross.

My Doing Good Journal
Doing Good Deed #50

Date Completed: _____

What did you learn from this experience?

_____

_____

_____

_____

_____

_____

_____

_____

Doing Good Deed #51:

Donate supplies to the Ronald McDonald House.

(www.rmhc.org)

My Doing Good Journal
Doing Good Deed #51

Date Completed: _____

What did you learn from this experience?

_____

_____

_____

_____

_____

_____

_____

_____

Doing Good Deed #52:

Give gift cards or bottles of water to your local sanitation workers and thank them.

My Doing Good Journal
Doing Good Deed #52

Date Completed: _____

What did you learn from this experience?

_____

_____

_____

_____

_____

_____

_____

_____

Doing Good Deed #53:

Offer to pet sit for a friend or neighbor going out of town.

My Doing Good Journal
Doing Good Deed #53

Date Completed: _____

What did you learn from this experience?

_____

_____

_____

_____

_____

_____

_____

_____

Doing Good Deed #54:

Donate laundry supplies to a patron at a local laundromat.

My Doing Good Journal
Doing Good Deed #54

Date Completed: _____

What did you learn from this experience?

_____

_____

_____

_____

_____

_____

_____

_____

Doing Good Deed #55:

Donate a good book to a correctional facility.

www.BooksThroughBars.org

(Books Through Bars)

My Doing Good Journal
Doing Good Deed #55

Date Completed: _____

What did you learn from this experience?

_____

_____

_____

_____

_____

_____

_____

_____

Doing Good Deed #56:

Smile at everyone you pass today and ask a few people about their day.

My Doing Good Journal
Doing Good Deed #56

Date Completed: _____

What did you learn from this experience?

_____

_____

_____

_____

_____

_____

_____

_____

Doing Good Deed #57:

Pass on a good book after you've read it.

My Doing Good Journal
Doing Good Deed #57

Date Completed: _____

What did you learn from this experience?

_____

_____

_____

_____

_____

_____

_____

_____

Doing Good Deed #58:

Volunteer to help wrap gifts for a charitable organization during the holidays.

My Doing Good Journal
Doing Good Deed #58

Date Completed: _____

What did you learn from this experience?

_____

_____

_____

_____

_____

_____

_____

_____

Doing Good Deed #59:

Offer to play games with someone living in a retirement home.

My Doing Good Journal
Doing Good Deed #59

Date Completed: _____

What did you learn from this experience?

_____

_____

_____

_____

_____

_____

_____

_____

Doing Good Deed #60:

Send a "thank you" note to your local police department.

My Doing Good Journal
Doing Good Deed #60

Date Completed: _____

What did you learn from this experience?

_____

_____

_____

_____

_____

_____

_____

_____

Doing Good Deed #61:

Volunteer your time at a local animal shelter.

My Doing Good Journal
Doing Good Deed #61

Date Completed: _____

What did you learn from this experience?

_____

_____

_____

_____

_____

_____

_____

Doing Good Deed #62:

Write a 'thank you' note of appreciation to your mail carrier.

My Doing Good Journal
Doing Good Deed #62

Date Completed: _____

What did you learn from this experience?

_____

_____

_____

_____

_____

_____

_____

_____

Doing Good Deed #63:

Collect deodorant and shampoo and donate them to a rehabilitation center for teens.

My Doing Good Journal
Doing Good Deed #63

Date Completed: _____

What did you learn from this experience?

_____

_____

_____

_____

_____

_____

_____

_____

Doing Good Deed #64:

Buy a prepaid phone or phone card and donate it to a homeless person or shelter.

My Doing Good Journal
Doing Good Deed #64

Date Completed: _____

What did you learn from this experience?

_____

_____

_____

_____

_____

_____

_____

Doing Good Deed #65:

Take flowers or candy to the staff at a local hospital.

My Doing Good Journal
Doing Good Deed #65

Date Completed: _____

What did you learn from this experience?

_____

_____

_____

_____

_____

_____

_____

_____

Doing Good Deed #66:

Leave a kind encouraging note on a receipt at a restaurant.

My Doing Good Journal
Doing Good Deed #66

Date Completed: _____

What did you learn from this experience?

_____

_____

_____

_____

_____

_____

_____

_____

Doing Good Deed #67:

Make arrangements to pay for a someone's gas or utility bill.

My Doing Good Journal
Doing Good Deed #67

Date Completed: _____

What did you learn from this experience?

_____

_____

_____

_____

_____

_____

_____

_____

Doing Good Deed #68:

Make sandwiches and deliver them to a homeless shelter.

My Doing Good Journal
Doing Good Deed #68

Date Completed: _____

What did you learn from this experience?

_____

_____

_____

_____

_____

_____

_____

_____

_____

Doing Good Deed #69:

Pay for movie tickets for a family while at the movie theater.

My Doing Good Journal
Doing Good Deed #69

Date Completed: _____

What did you learn from this experience?

_____

_____

_____

_____

_____

_____

_____

_____

Doing Good Deed #70:

Donate gently used electronics to a charitable organization.

My Doing Good Journal
Doing Good Deed #70

Date Completed: _____

What did you learn from this experience?

_____

_____

_____

_____

_____

_____

_____

_____

Doing Good Deed #71:

Organize transportation for those who cannot drive to help them get to the polls on voting day.

My Doing Good Journal
Doing Good Deed #71

Date Completed: _____

What did you learn from this experience?

_____

_____

_____

_____

_____

_____

_____

_____

Doing Good Deed #72:

Donate crayons and coloring books to a children's ward at a local hospital.

My Doing Good Journal
Doing Good Deed #72

Date Completed: _____

What did you learn from this experience?

_____

_____

_____

_____

_____

_____

_____

_____

Doing Good Deed #73:

Volunteer to repaint your local park benches through your local government.

My Doing Good Journal
Doing Good Deed #73

Date Completed: _____

What did you learn from this experience?

_____

_____

_____

_____

_____

_____

_____

_____

Doing Good Deed #74:

Identify and encourage five young people to register to vote.

(www.RockTheVote.org)

My Doing Good Journal
Doing Good Deed #74

Date Completed: _____

What did you learn from this experience?

_____

_____

_____

_____

_____

_____

_____

_____

Doing Good Deed #75:

Donate professional attire to organizations like "Suited for Change" or "Dress for Success".

(www.suitedforchange.org)

or

(www.dressforsuccess.org)

My Doing Good Journal
Doing Good Deed #75

Date Completed: _____

What did you learn from this experience?

_____

_____

_____

_____

_____

_____

_____

Doing Good Deed #76:

Donate new pajamas to a program that helps foster kids.

My Doing Good Journal
Doing Good Deed #76

Date Completed: _____

What did you learn from this experience?

_____

_____

_____

_____

_____

_____

_____

_____

Doing Good Deed #77:

Deliver a turkey dinner to a family in need for Thanksgiving.

My Doing Good Journal
Doing Good Deed #77

Date Completed: _____

What did you learn from this experience?

_____

_____

_____

_____

_____

_____

_____

_____

Doing Good Deed #78:

Deliver baked goods to a nursing or retirement home during the holiday season.

My Doing Good Journal
Doing Good Deed #78

Date Completed: _____

What did you learn from this experience?

_____

_____

_____

_____

_____

_____

_____

_____

Doing Good Deed #79:

Donate a magazine subscription to an HIV/AIDS clinic.

My Doing Good Journal
Doing Good Deed #79

Date Completed: _____

What did you learn from this experience?

_____

_____

_____

_____

_____

_____

_____

_____

Doing Good Deed #80:

Become CPR certified. You never know whose life you may save.

My Doing Good Journal
Doing Good Deed #80

Date Completed: _____

What did you learn from this experience?

_____

_____

_____

_____

_____

_____

_____

_____

Doing Good Deed #81:

Give a gift card to a janitor.

My Doing Good Journal
Doing Good Deed #81

Date Completed: _____

What did you learn from this experience?

_____

_____

_____

_____

_____

_____

_____

_____

Doing Good Deed #82:

Send a teacher a "thank you" gift.

My Doing Good Journal
Doing Good Deed #82

Date Completed: _____

What did you learn from this experience?

_____

_____

_____

_____

_____

_____

_____

Doing Good Deed #83:

Plant a tree!

My Doing Good Journal
Doing Good Deed #83

Date Completed: _____

What did you learn from this experience?

_____

_____

_____

_____

_____

_____

_____

_____

Doing Good Deed #84:

Make a payment toward a stranger's layaway fees.

My Doing Good Journal
Doing Good Deed #84

Date Completed: _____

What did you learn from this experience?

_____

_____

_____

_____

_____

_____

_____

_____

Doing Good Deed #85:

Create and deliver personalized cards to patients in a hospital.

My Doing Good Journal
Doing Good Deed #85

Date Completed: _____

What did you learn from this experience?

_____

_____

_____

_____

_____

_____

_____

Doing Good Deed #86:

Volunteer to build a house with Habitat for Humanity.

My Doing Good Journal
Doing Good Deed #86

Date Completed: _____

What did you learn from this experience?

_____

_____

_____

_____

_____

_____

_____

_____

Doing Good Deed #87:

Donate your hair to Locks of Love.

www.locksoflove.org

My Doing Good Journal
Doing Good Deed #87

Date Completed: _____

What did you learn from this experience?

_____

_____

_____

_____

_____

_____

_____

_____

Doing Good Deed #88:

Buy dessert for your server at a restaurant.

My Doing Good Journal
Doing Good Deed #88

Date Completed: _____

What did you learn from this experience?

_____

_____

_____

_____

_____

_____

_____

_____

Doing Good Deed #89:

Offer your seat to an elderly, pregnant or disabled person.

My Doing Good Journal
Doing Good Deed #89

Date Completed: _____

What did you learn from this experience?

_____

_____

_____

_____

_____

_____

_____

_____

Doing Good Deed #90:

Mow the lawn or rake leaves for a neighbor.

My Doing Good Journal
Doing Good Deed #90

Date Completed: _____

What did you learn from this experience?

_____

_____

_____

_____

_____

_____

_____

_____

Doing Good Deed #91:

Pay for a stranger's public transportation fare.

My Doing Good Journal
Doing Good Deed #91

Date Completed: _____

What did you learn from this experience?

_____

_____

_____

_____

_____

_____

_____

_____

Doing Good Deed #92:

Leave notes of encouragement on people's cars.

My Doing Good Journal
Doing Good Deed #92

Date Completed: _____

What did you learn from this experience?

_____

_____

_____

_____

_____

_____

_____

_____

Doing Good Deed #93:

Make a donation to "Toys for Tots".

www.ToysforTots.org

My Doing Good Journal
Doing Good Deed #93

Date Completed: _____

What did you learn from this experience?

_____

_____

_____

_____

_____

_____

_____

_____

Doing Good Deed #94:

Use your time, talent, and treasure to show the love of Jesus Christ.

My Doing Good Journal
Doing Good Deed #94

Date Completed: _____

What did you learn from this experience?

_____

_____

_____

_____

_____

_____

_____

_____

Doing Good Deed #95:

Volunteer your time to help sort goods at a local food pantry.

My Doing Good Journal
Doing Good Deed #95

Date Completed: _____

What did you learn from this experience?

_____

_____

_____

_____

_____

_____

_____

_____

Doing Good Deed #96:

Treat a friend to lunch or dinner.

My Doing Good Journal
Doing Good Deed #96

Date Completed: _____

What did you learn from this experience?

_____

_____

_____

_____

_____

_____

_____

_____

Doing Good Deed #97:

Donate gently used coats to a charity during the winter season.

My Doing Good Journal
Doing Good Deed #97

Date Completed: _____

What did you learn from this experience?

_____

_____

_____

_____

_____

_____

_____

_____

Doing Good Deed #98:

Volunteer to clean up a foster home or community center.

My Doing Good Journal
Doing Good Deed #98

Date Completed: _____

What did you learn from this experience?

_____

_____

_____

_____

_____

_____

_____

_____

Doing Good Deed #99:

Organize an undergarment drive for a women's shelter.

My Doing Good Journal
Doing Good Deed #99

Date Completed: _____

What did you learn from this experience?

_____

_____

_____

_____

_____

_____

_____

_____

Doing Good Deed #100:

Buy this book for someone you love to help us change the world, one good deed at a time!

My Doing Good Journal
Doing Good Deed #100

Date Completed: _____

What did you learn from this experience?

_____

_____

_____

_____

_____

_____

_____

_____

Doing Good
Is A Way Of Life

For more information on doing good and giving back, visit our website: www.DoingGood.com

Date Completed Book: _____

How will you commit to changing the world?

_____

_____

_____

Share your thoughts with us at info@thestaffordfoundation.org